MW01234857

IMAGES
of America

HISTORIC CHARLESTON
GARDENS

A Garden in Charleston

During the Victorian Era, classical garden styles gave way to more fanciful, romantic designs. In this scene published in a popular 19th-century book entitled *Picturesque America*, a Charleston garden has been remade in the style of the day and features elaborately pruned shrubbery, walks lined with conch shells, and the South Carolina state tree, the palmetto, prominently located off-center on the lawn. (Courtesy of *Picturesque America*.)

ON THE COVER: A group of young boys enjoys sailing their boats in a fountain at Hampton Park in the 1950s. The park, built on the site of Charleston's Inter-State and West-Indian Exposition, became a very popular public garden for the city and contained a zoo and band shell as well as flower-bordered and tree-shaded paths. (Photograph by J. R. Burbage; courtesy of the *Post and Courier*.)

IMAGES
of America

HISTORIC CHARLESTON
GARDENS

T. Hunter McEaddy
and Catherine P. McEaddy

ARCADIA
PUBLISHING

Published by Arcadia Publishing
Charleston SC, Chicago IL, Portsmouth NH, San Francisco CA

Library of Congress Catalog Card Number: 2007924740

For all general information contact Arcadia Publishing at:
Telephone 843-853-2070
Fax 843-853-0044
E-mail sales@arcadiapublishing.com
For customer service and orders:
Toll-Free 1-888-313-2665

Visit us on the Internet at www.arcadiapublishing.com

CONTENTS

ACKNOWLEDGMENTS

We must first acknowledge the generosity and support of a number of Charlestonians who shared their family photo albums and, in so doing, provided the foundation for this book. They include Gale Belser Thompson, Lorraine and Frank Hanckel, Charlotte and Strait Fairey, Susanne and Tom Trainer, Eva Ravenel, and Randy Pelzer. A heartfelt thanks to them, our own family, and many other friends whose enthusiasm for this project and encouragement never flagged, even when, on occasion, ours did. Also we thank Katherine Robinson and Karen Emmons of the Historic Charleston Foundation and Robert Gurley of the Preservation Society of Charleston, all of whom gave access and guidance in navigating the priceless archives held in their respective organizations. We are also grateful to the *Post and Courier* for permitting us to use our cover photograph as well as other images and to the Library of Congress for the incredible treasure trove of images they have made available to all.

At Arcadia Publishing, our editors, Maggie Tiller Bullwinkel and Adam Ferrell, have done their jobs with both patience and professionalism, meaning they spoke both softly and firmly as needed to keep the authors on task. Jaquelin Pelzer, formerly a publisher with Arcadia, deserves special credit for thinking of us and bringing us together with our publisher when the idea for this book was first conceived.

Finally we want to acknowledge the gardeners of Charleston from generations past, whose works and hobbies we celebrate here, and the photographers who recorded their efforts and thereby made it possible for us to share this wonderful legacy. To all of these, past and present, and to others, of whose contributions we may not be aware, we say a heartfelt "thank you!"

INTRODUCTION

In 1670, the founders of Charleston established their first settlement on the western bank of the Ashley River across from the present-day city. No doubt, the first task of these pioneers was to clear the wilderness and plant gardens for sustenance and perhaps for a bit of pleasure as well. Today this original settlement is the location of Charles Towne Landing, a state park surrounded by suburbia, and visitors can visit a replica of the community where these earliest Charleston gardeners lived.

After some 10 years, the settlement moved across the river to a low-lying peninsula facing a large harbor formed by the convergence of the Ashley and Cooper Rivers with a distant view of the Atlantic Ocean. On this site, over the next three centuries, Charleston and her gardens would begin and evolve into the historic city known around the world, not only for her priceless architecture but also for her gardens and gardening tradition. Indeed, today in the 21st century, the gardens of Charleston, both private and public, are celebrated and documented as never before, and they are a year-round source of delight for citizens and visitors alike.

Ordinary private gardens of downtown Charleston, the old city on the peninsula, form the majority of the images in this book. They say much about the gardening tastes of their owners, changing economics, the passage of time, and the lives of Charlestonians who lived with them as an everyday part of the cityscape. They are ordinary only in the sense that they did not achieve individual fame, but collectively, they are extraordinary for they form the bulk of landscape for which this city of gardens is justly famous.

Geography and climate certainly contribute to Charleston's garden fame. Through the centuries, a rich garden soil has built up layer-by-layer over what was originally, in many areas, a low sandy or marshy peninsula. Warm ocean waters have contributed to a climate with mild temperatures and a long growing season where vines and weeds plus imported exotic plants from around the world have thrived as surely as native palms, oaks, and pines. No doubt, these circumstances seem to have brought out the gardener in nearly everyone fortunate enough to call Charleston home.

What Charlestonians refer to as piazzas, the rest of the world may know as porches or verandas, but this distinctive term is almost universally applied to those indoor/outdoor spaces gracing the vast majority of homes as well as many public and commercial buildings in the city. Piazzas are an architectural response to what many would say is Charleston's only significant natural downside—long, hot, and humid summers persisting for almost half of every year can temper the enthusiasm of even the heartiest native.

In the late 17th and early 18th centuries, the architecture of Charleston tended to follow European precedents, and examples of this period before piazzas remain today. Piazzas began to appear, however, as architecture became more responsive to local conditions. Indeed, the Charleston single house, the city's quintessential domestic architectural type, features piazzas as links between house and garden, virtually serving as garden rooms, where much of life in the Charleston garden actually occurs.

It is a quickly discernible fact that much of the character of the Charleston cityscape and its gardens comes not from the lush, sub-tropical, natural greenery but from the man-made features of the gardens that enclose and punctuate them. Most lots in the old city are small by suburban standards and nearly all are filled with the footprints of buildings, with the remaining space typically surrounded by walls, gates, and other entrances.

Many of these are objects of considerable beauty and distinctive style that enhance the character of the gardens they enclose. Through the centuries, tastes have evolved so that the earliest tall, solid brick and stucco walls, now often growing their own gardens of moss and ferns, have given way to more open, wrought-iron and even wooden picket fences and those with combinations of materials. The ironwork of Charleston has reached the level of fine art, and many of the city's gardens are graced with handsome examples, as these images attest.

Although large residential lots certainly exist, the majority of Charleston's gardens are rather small and confined by most standards. It is perhaps for this reason that outdoor life has never been confined to private gardens. Indeed, the street life of the city and its public spaces, parks, and gardens have always provided essential breathing room.

City parks, such as White Point Gardens at the foot of the peninsula and Hampton Park near its northern boundary, as well as the public promenades facing the harbor and rivers along High Battery and Murray Boulevard, have long served as public gardens. Charlestonians have gathered in these places to stroll, visit, fish and shrimp, and enjoy the company of friends and family and the beauty of natural surroundings beyond their private realms.

For most of its history, Charleston was a small city on a peninsula surrounded by its rivers, its harbor, and across from these, countryside on the bordering mainland and sea islands. Indeed, it was not until the middle of the 20th century that suburban development began to sprawl beyond the rivers. Before that time, these rural lands were home to plantations and farms. Farther out, Sullivan's Island, the Isle of Palms, and Edisto Island were home to summer cottages. For generations, Charlestonians sought to escape the heat of midsummer for these more comfortable climes.

As the images in the final chapter attest, gardening enthusiasm was more sporadic in these retreats. Certainly gardens existed in the countryside, especially where they were part of full-time residences, and Charleston's world-famous plantation gardens, open to the public, were a definite exception. In many rural retreats, however, and certainly at the beaches, the predominant gardening philosophy seems to have been to "let nature take its course."

Few products of design are less permanent than gardens. Nature causes them to grow and change from their beginnings, and shifting tastes, uses, and ownership all play their part in affecting this change. Thus the gardens of today, unless intentionally re-created for historic purposes, may reflect some aspects of their past, but they are not what they were in the past. While the grand gardens of contemporary Charleston are recorded and celebrated in a number of beautiful publications, those of past centuries, and especially the ordinary residential gardens, are generally unknown today. *Historic Charleston Gardens* brings together, from archives and family albums, a photographic record of a small sample of the city's gardens and those who created them, lived in them, and loved them from 50 to 150 years ago. It is only a sample, and the authors have no doubt that many more photographs are waiting to be discovered.

One

RESIDENTIAL GARDENS OF DOWNTOWN CHARLESTON

In 1880, Charlestonians, as in years past and future, would stroll along the High Battery. This outing provided opportunity to view the gardens of the mansions lining East Battery Street while enjoying cooling breezes from the harbor. (Wood engraving after sketch by Walter Goater, Frank Leslie, publisher; courtesy of the Library of Congress, Prints and Photographs Division.)

The Manigault House at Wragg Square and Meeting Street is pictured undergoing restoration and showing a varied collection of plants and trees either remaining from a previous garden or volunteering in the favorable growing conditions found in Charleston. After work was completed, a more formal garden layout, which included boxwood, camellias, oleander, and yucca, surrounds a lawn panel bordered by paths that grace the property, which is now operated as a museum. (Photographs by Louis Schwartz; courtesy of Historic Charleston Foundation.)

A rare snowfall in 1941 covers one of the new gardens on the lower peninsula facing the Ashley River on landfill created following construction of the Murray Boulevard seawall in 1910. (Courtesy of Charlotte and Strait Fairey.)

An early-20th-century house facing Colonial Lake provides an unusual setting for a garden in a 19th-century neighborhood. The house is suburban in architectural style, and the garden is laid out with unusual raised terraces, rather than the more traditional gardens of its neighbors. (Photograph by Franklin Frost Sams; courtesy of Historic Charleston Foundation.)

In 1865, a South Battery Street home is shown after it was commandeered for the headquarters of Union general John P. Hatch and occupying forces following the fall of Charleston. Evidence of the former owner's garden is visible along the block. (Courtesy of Library of Congress, Prints and Photographs Division.)

General Hatch and his staff are shown posing on the steps of the South Battery Street home that served as his headquarters during the occupation of Charleston by the Union army in 1865. Little evidence remains of the plants visible from the street in the previous view. (Courtesy of Library of Congress, Prints and Photographs Division.)

This former dependency of the famed Sword Gate House at 32 Legare Street is shown in the 1950s after the property had been subdivided and given a new address on Tradd Street. The upper floors were used as a private residence while the ground level had been converted to use as a bed-and-breakfast and garden space reduced to a minimum to accommodate guest parking. (Photograph by Louis I. Schwartz; courtesy of Library of Congress, Prints and Photograph Division, Historic American Buildings Survey.)

A privy was a necessary part of any house before the days of indoor plumbing. They were generally placed in the rear garden and were often attractive structures in the finer homes such as this example at the Daniel Huger House, 54 Meeting Street. (Photograph by Charles N. Bayless, AIA; courtesy of Library of Congress, Prints and Photographs Division, Historic American Buildings Survey.)

This home was reportedly in the process of being relocated from Franklin Street to Broad Street on log rollers. No doubt, a new garden was in its future. (Photograph by Franklin Frost Sams; courtesy of Historic Charleston Foundation.)

Another Victorian-era structure, located at the corner of Meeting Street and South Battery Street facing White Point Gardens, has a large fenced yard with ample room for a future garden but no evidence of planting in this early view. (Photograph by *Art Work of Charleston*, W. H. Parish, publisher; courtesy of Historic Charleston Foundation.)

A scattering of sparse plantings is all that remains to suggest a former garden at 72 Anson Street. Gardens are indeed fragile and will disappear over time if not tended. (Photograph by Louis Schwartz; courtesy of Historic Charleston Foundation.)

An 1865 view shows the rubble where one home had stood and the barren landscape surrounding a second at 180 Broad Street. Both the homes and gardens of Charleston suffered from neglect, damage, and destruction during the Civil War years. (Courtesy of Library of Congress, Prints and Photographs Division.)

An 1865 photograph taken from the roof of the Orphan House shows the Citadel in its original Marion Square location, the distant steeple of the Second Presbyterian Church, and homes in the foreground whose gardens appear to have been turned over to food production during the war years. (Courtesy of Library of Congress, Prints and Photographs Division.)

In the first decades of the 20th century, suburban development spread up the peninsula to Hampton Park, formerly the site of the Charleston Inter-State and West Indian Exposition in 1901. Before that, it was the location of the antebellum Washington Race Course. Relocation of the Citadel campus also encouraged neighborhood growth. The home was located on Elmwood Avenue between Huger and Moultrie Streets. It appears the family cow not only provided milk but also served as a pet for the children at this birthday party. (Courtesy of Historic Charleston Foundation, Eberle Collection.)

A young cowboy enjoys the wide-open spaces at 30 Parkwood Avenue in the 1950s. By this time, the neighborhood trees and shrubs had reached a level of maturity that gave the Hampton Park neighborhood an established appearance. Although gardeners in these newer areas had more room for lawns and gardens, their choices for plants were not all that different as local taste in plant material, and climate continued to be a major influence. One exception was that larger plantings of large azaleas became more common with room to spread out. (Courtesy of Historic Charleston Foundation, Eberle Collection.)

The 18th-century home at 8 South Battery Street, known as the William Washington House, featured a formal garden to the left and informal plantings to the right in this 19th-century view. Varieties of small street trees, including live oaks, a crepe myrtle, and a palmetto, have been planted along the city sidewalk in front. (Photograph by Lanneau's Art Store, publisher; courtesy of Historic Charleston Foundation.)

The mid-18th-century Thomas Heyward House at 87 Church Street had a re-created formal garden in 1940, although volunteer native vines appear to cover the roofs and walls of two dependencies. (Photograph by C. O. Greene; courtesy of Library of Congress, Prints and Photographs Division, Historic American Buildings Survey.)

A photograph of an early-19th-century building containing three dwellings overlooks lush gardens to the rear and a view beyond to Charleston Harbor. It is unusual in that the building contains three separate homes with the three small, walled gardens side by side. (Photograph by Charles N. Bayless; courtesy of Historic Charleston Foundation.)

This Victorian residence at 152 Broad Street is shown in the first years of the 20th century with a simple garden consisting of foundation plantings and a lawn panel surrounded by an iron picket fence. Even old gardens were once new. (Photograph by Franklin Frost Sams; courtesy of Historic Charleston Foundation.)

This street scene, c. 1940, shows two double houses each flanked by a single house. The double house style, with piazzas, provides opportunities for gardens facing the street when the buildings are set back from the sidewalks. These homeowners took advantage of the space with planting that provided both privacy and shade. A variety of wooden fence styles separates these homes from the public sidewalks. (Photograph by William M. Muckenfuss; courtesy of Historic Charleston Foundation.)

Clearly a flower lover resided at this home in 1940. Informal plantings of blooming annuals and perennials fill the beds between narrow walkways, and a Lady Banksia rose climbs a pipe trellis built across a brick terrace. (Photograph by William M. Muckenfuss; courtesy of Historic Charleston Foundation.)

The large building in the background is Baker Sanatorium, a hospital located in an otherwise residential neighborhood. Various types of enclosures surround adjacent gardens, including stucco with pierced brick, wood with stucco, and all-wood pickets. Magnolia trees and a palmetto trunk are visible over the walls. (Photograph by Franklin Frost Sams; courtesy of Historic Charleston Foundation.)

Two generations in very different outfits enjoy their garden at the intersection of Fishburne and St. Philip Streets. (Courtesy of Historic Charleston Foundation, Eberle Collection.)

This mid-20th-century view shows a home and garden enthusiastically decked out to celebrate the Christmas season. Such exuberant holiday decorations became much more widespread toward the end of the century, even in the most conservative and historic sections of the city. (Photograph by William M. Muckenfuss; courtesy of Historic Charleston Foundation.)

This house sits well back from the street and provides space for a large front garden, which is unusual in Charleston. A young palmetto, the South Carolina state tree, appeared to have "volunteered" in the center. (Photograph by H. Philip Staats; courtesy of Historic Charleston Foundation.)

The Pink House, an 18th-century structure at 17 Chalmers Street, does not appear to have a garden. However, who knows what may lie to the rear where treetops are in evidence. Courtesy of Historic Charleston Foundation.)

This photograph of 46 Anson Street shows a typical, small courtyard, which began to grace former dependencies subdivided from larger properties in the 20th century. (Photograph by Balfour H. Walker; courtesy of Historic Charleston Foundation.)

This view shows a home under construction at 32 Coming Street, *c.* 1900, still leaving ample space for a future garden. (Courtesy of Historic Charleston Foundation.)

Love of gardening crosses many economic boundaries, and even modest homes often have gardens that flourish in the favorable growing conditions of Charleston. (Courtesy of Historic Charleston Foundation, Eberle Collection.)

A new brick wall conceals the garden of this home at 68 Anson Street. (Photograph by Louis Schwartz; courtesy of Historic Charleston Foundation.)

A large group of children enjoys a birthday party on the front lawn of this Elmwood Avenue home near the Citadel campus in this view from the middle of the 20th century. (Courtesy of Historic Charleston Foundation.)

Even small Charleston gardens still needed space reserved for off-street parking whenever possible and, of course, for domestic chores such as washing the family pup, as shown in this scene from the 1950s. (Courtesy of Lorraine and Frank Hanckel.)

This "garden" at 9 Fulton Street, shown in its last days in the mid-20th century, was soon to be replaced, along with its home, by a parking lot. A jungle of weeds and vines is never far behind when neglect sets in. (Courtesy of the Preservation Society of Charleston.)

This mid-20th-century view of a Victorian-era garden illustrates how the exotic plantings favored in the latter part of the 19th century had thrived in the long, sub-tropical growing seasons that Charleston enjoys. (Courtesy of the Preservation Society of Charleston.)

This mid-20th-century view of a Tradd Street residence shows an exuberant take-over by native vines and shrubs where a more formal garden probably existed in earlier times. (Courtesy of the Preservation Society of Charleston.)

Three ladies and their dog enjoy tea beside a vine-covered garden wall in this view of the garden at 64 South Battery from the early 20th century. The tablecloth, silver teapot, and vase of flowers suggest that they were accustomed to enjoying life in the garden. (Courtesy of Susanne and Tom Trainer.)

A garden at 7 Legare Street shows many elements commonly found in Charleston, including elaborate wrought-iron fencing; masonry columns, including one covered with fig vine; liriope or "monkey grass" bordering the walk; and a pittosporum in full spring bloom hanging over the wall. (Photograph by Charles N. Bayless; courtesy of Library of Congress, Prints and Photographs Division, Historic American Buildings Survey.)

A 19th-century bride and groom pose stiffly in a backyard on their wedding day. It seems odd that such an important picture would have been set in the decidedly informal rear yard where domestic chores typically occurred rather than in more attractive surroundings. To the right of the bride stands a joggling board, a popular bouncing bench found in many Charleston gardens. (Photograph by Franklin Frost Sams; courtesy of Historic Charleston Foundation.)

The William Rhett House, one of Charleston's oldest homes, was built in the early 18th century as a plantation house on the outskirts of the city. As development moved up the peninsula, the Ansonborough neighborhood grew up around it. In these views, taken in the 1950s, the home had deteriorated badly, but it was subsequently restored. As a result, a small planting area in front was lost, but a handsome garden was created on a sizable portion of the lot to the left. (Above and below courtesy of Historic Charleston Foundation.)

Here is one of a group of row houses dating to the 18th century facing East Bay Street south of Broad, popularly known today as "Rainbow Row" because of their bright colors. These homes meet the sidewalk, but many have elegant courtyard gardens. (Photograph by H. Philip Staats; courtesy of Historic Charleston Foundation.)

"Summertime and the livin' is easy" in this mid-20th-century garden south of Broad Street. Though many Charlestonians fled the city heat and humidity for the beaches or the mountains whenever possible, gardens remained an alternative for those left behind. (Courtesy of Eva Ravenel.)

An 1865 view of 48 Elizabeth Street shows a large mansion built as the city spread northward up the peninsula in the 19th century. Residence of Gov. William Aiken, the antebellum home and outbuildings occupied much of the property. A small garden fronted the two-story piazzas, and the remainder of the property to the rear was taken up with a paved courtyard surrounded by servants' quarters, stables, a kitchen building, and other domestic facilities. (Courtesy of Library of Congress, Prints and Photographs Division.)

The former home of Gov. William Aiken at 48 Elizabeth Street was built between 1817 and 1825 and occupies a large lot of about 90 feet by 320 feet. While an ornamental garden fronted the south-facing piazzas, the rear courtyard was lined with stables, servants' quarters, and other domestic conveniences. (Photograph by Charles N. Bayless, AIA; courtesy of Library of Congress, Prints and Photographs Division, Historic American Buildings Survey.)

The William Blacklock House on Bull Street in Harleston Village, a Charleston neighborhood, was constructed in the early 19th century. By the 1950s and 1960s, when these pictures were taken, the garden to the rear of the house had evolved into a lawn spotted with trees and clipped evergreen shrubbery. Prominent features that survived from the original garden were dependencies including servants' quarters and a small, brick summerhouse with Gothic arches. Small structures such as this were often features of the finer gardens and provided points of interests as well as shelter for enjoying the outdoors. (Photographs by Louis I. Schwartz; courtesy of Library of Congress, Prints and Photographs Division, Historic American Buildings Survey.)

A young boy and his pet goat enjoyed a wide lawn and an ornamental pool lined with decorative concrete borders at 14 Elmwood Avenue in the early 1920s. Boxwood lines the iron picket fence and a Model T Ford appears through the shrubs. (Courtesy of Historic Charleston Foundation, Eberle Collection.)

A new garden has just begun along with the restoration of an old single house in the Ansonborough neighborhood of Charleston. A large clump of oleander is seen at the corner of the piazza. (Photograph by Louis Schwartz; courtesy of Historic Charleston Foundation.)

A light snowfall in 1942 covers the evergreen hedge and small trees fronting 20 Kenilworth Avenue. The side yard contains an elaborate trellis and arbor, which probably supported vines for shade and privacy during the growing season. (Courtesy of Historic Charleston Foundation, Eberle Collection.)

A group of children poses in their Sunday or party best on the open lawn of this Hampton Park Terrace garden. Behind the hedge is a home on Huger Street. (Courtesy of Historic Charleston Foundation, Eberle Collection.)

A mother and her children admire the flowers in a garden on Murray Boulevard in the early 1960s. As elsewhere, a love of gardening is passed down from generation to generation, and gardening traditions continue to flourish in the 21st century. (Courtesy of Gale Belser Thompson.)

By the middle of the 20th century, many Charleston gardens featured mostly winter- and spring-blooming shrubbery, such as azaleas and camellias. Large displays of flowering annuals and perennials such as these were less common as they flourished in the summer when many gardeners fled the heat of the city. (Courtesy of Gale Belser Thompson.)

These boys do not appear to admire the beautiful camellia bloom as much as most Charlestonians. These handsome shrubs, a favorite since the 18th century, brighten gardens with large, colorful blooms from late fall through the winter months to early spring when such showy displays are a welcome, if rare, occurrence. (Courtesy of Gale Belser Thompson.)

A young girl poses in her mid-20th-century Sunday best in a small courtyard on King Street. Even the smallest space could be captured for a touch of color and an interesting brick arch as a focal point on the garden wall. (Courtesy of Gale Belser Thompson.)

An ancient brick wall, a birdbath with a small statue, and brick-bordered planting beds were examples of widely used garden features in Charleston gardens by the middle of the 20th century. (Courtesy of Gale Belser Thompson.)

A raised, slate terrace bordered in reclaimed, old English brick provides a comfortable spot to relax and enjoy a garden south of Broad Street. (Courtesy of Gale Belser Thompson.)

A great deal could happen in a very small Charleston garden filled with flowers, vines, a fountain, and a proud gardener posing with her handiwork. (Courtesy of Gale Belser Thompson.)

This view of a Tradd Street residence shows typical planting not often visible from the street. Dependencies such as former carriage and kitchen houses at the rear of such properties often received extensions of the garden along the side piazzas of the main residences once they were no longer required as areas for domestic activities in the 20th century. (Courtesy of the Preservation Society of Charleston.)

This extremely elaborate Victorian residence was unusual for Charleston. Located at 12 Legare Street at the corner of Gibbes Street, the house appears to fill most of the lot, although there is evidence of a small garden at the left of the photograph. (Photograph by *Art Work of Charleston*, W. H. Parish, publisher; courtesy of Historic Charleston Foundation.)

A young girl, apparently in costume from earlier days, poses with her pet dog against the background of 518 Huger Street. The open space, broad lawns and lots large enough to accommodate freestanding garages and servants' quarters were all departures from earlier Charleston gardens and were not unlike the homes and gardens of other communities in this newer area near Hampton Park. (Courtesy of Historic Charleston Foundation, Eberle Collection.)

Two toddlers smiled at the camera in the rear yard of 15 Kenilworth Avenue in the Hampton Park neighborhood. It appears that any gardening did not extend to this portion of the property, which shows only a clothesline, chicken yard, and shed. (Courtesy of Historic Charleston Foundation, Eberle Collection.)

The large Victorian mansion at 149 Wentworth Street appeared newly constructed when this photograph was taken. Only small trees were visible behind the garden fence, although a greenhouse to the right suggests that a garden lover resided at the property. (Photograph by *Art Work of Charleston*, W. H. Parish, publisher; courtesy of Historic Charleston Foundation.)

A girl graduate poses in the family garden on State Street in downtown Charleston in this view from the 1940s. Clearly someone in the family loved flowers, and this made a pleasant setting for recording one of life's special events. (Courtesy of Lorraine and Frank Hanckel.)

This home on lower Meeting Street is one of several extremely large and ornate structures built after the War Between the States. Unusual garden features include the tall yucca plants, vine-covered arbors, and a striking glass-roofed conservatory to the rear. (Photograph by *Art Work of Charleston*, W. H. Parish, publisher; courtesy of Historic Charleston Foundation.)

A profusion of palmettos of all sizes appears to be a tropical jungle at the corner of South and East Battery Streets in this 1950s photograph. Palmettos, a palm native to South Carolina, will grow without encouragement, especially along the coastal areas of the state. (Courtesy of Historic Charleston Foundation.)

A baby, a dog, and an automobile complete this scene of open lawns and shade trees in this 1920s photograph set in the Hampton Park neighborhood. (Courtesy of Historic Charleston Foundation, Eberle Collection.)

Reflections of its former glory remain in the form of assorted plants and climbing roses on trellises at 2 Amherst Street at the corner of East Bay Street. The original Cooper River Bridge is visible to the right in this view from the 1940s. (Courtesy of Historic Charleston Foundation.)

The Christopher Belser House, a grand structure built in 1800 at the corner of Amherst and East Bay Streets, had lost its former garden in favor of a play yard by the 1950s. Such was the fate of many homes in neighborhoods that had gone into decline, although some, including this one, have since been restored. (Photograph by Louis I. Schwartz; courtesy of Library of Congress, Prints and Photograph Division, Historic American Buildings Survey.)

Before the creation of Murray Boulevard, this late-18th-century South Battery Street residence had a much smaller garden along the edge of Lenwood Creek and the Ashley River marshes. The 1910 landfill behind the new seawall not only created many new building lots but also expanded existing properties formerly located along the water's edge. This view (above) from the 1930s showed a much larger garden built over the new landfill, which dramatically altered the original. Subsequently this was replaced with a modern, rear addition to the house and a kidney-shaped swimming pool, as shown in the below photograph taken in the 1970s. This garden is an excellent example of how changing tastes and usage contribute to gardening being one of the least-permanent art forms. (Above photograph courtesy of Randy Pelzer. Below photograph by Charles N. Bayless, AIA; courtesy of Library of Congress, Prints and Photographs Division, Historic American Buildings Survey.)

This Victorian house, built at 170 Broad Street in the latter 19th century, contrasts with its older, single house neighbor not only in architectural style but also in its placement on the lot. The site allowed both a front and side garden along with separate piazzas. Pipe trellises supported vines and provided shade. Young street trees were planted along the city sidewalk, and the property was surrounded by an iron picket fence typical of the era. (Photograph by *Art Work of Charleston*, W. H. Parish, publisher; courtesy of Historic Charleston Foundation.)

A gathering of neighborhood children is pictured fishing in a pool, showing once again how many aspects of family life took place in the gardens of Charleston in the days before air-conditioning and television. (Photograph by J. R. Burbage; courtesy of the *Post and Courier*.)

An open lawn on lower Church Street where one might expect a formal parterre garden was not uncommon and provided ample play space in this 1940s scene. (Courtesy of Eva Ravenel.)

This 1970s view shows remnants of a former garden including a large rose arbor at the Gov. Thomas Bennett house built in 1811. Subsequently a formal garden, deemed appropriate to the period of the property but also designed to accommodate contemporary entertaining, was developed. (Photograph by Charles N. Bayless, AIA; courtesy of Library of Congress, Prints and Photographs Division, Historic American Buildings Survey.)

Although the neighborhood South of Broad is traditionally thought of as having the city's most elegant homes and gardens, in the 18th and early 19th centuries, many of Charleston's grandest residences and largest properties began to be built north and west on the peninsula as suburban development expanded beyond the original city fortifications. Located several blocks above Calhoun Street, this home on Thomas Street was situated well back from the street in a lush garden surrounded by an ornate, wrought-iron fence with gates opening to a semi-circular carriage drive. (Photograph by Clarke Photo; courtesy of Frank and Lorraine Hanckel.)

This large, handsome home at the corner of Thomas and Vanderhorst Streets was the city residence of the Hanckel family, who also owned the Coburg Dairy west of the Ashley River. Its large site contained an elaborate garden with a variety of plants and statuary and featured a circular carriage drive that connected to the street through two tall, wrought-iron gates and a picket fence that enclosed the garden. (Photograph by Lanneau's Art Store, publisher; courtesy of Frank and Lorraine Hanckel.)

Small evergreen trees filled the entrance garden and partially obscured the 18th-century Miles Brewton House on lower King Street. A large garden, not visible in this view, filled the property to the rear. Wooden barriers protected newly planted street trees, and the vacant lot in the foreground suggests that a previous neighboring house had been destroyed. (Photograph by W. B. Austin; courtesy of Historic Charleston Foundation.)

By 1938, the rear garden of the Miles Brewton House, a handsome Georgian mansion built in the 1760s at 27 King Street, had become a profusion of trees, shrubs, and vines. (Photograph by John P. O'Neill; courtesy of Library of Congress, Prints and Photographs Division, Historic American Buildings Survey.)

In this view of the rear garden of the 18th-century Miles Brewton House at 27 King Street, the garden appears overgrown. In the latter part of the 20th century, it was restored to an 18th-century appearance with walkways and parterres. (Photograph by H. Philip Staats; courtesy of Historic Charleston Foundation.)

A somewhat careworn dependency is shown in the overgrown garden at 27 King Street. Buildings such as this might have been an office, a summer house, or an elaborate privy. (Photograph by H. Philip Staats; courtesy of Historic Charleston Foundation.)

A view taken c. 1938 from the roof of the Old City Jail shows a neighborhood of formerly substantial, 19th-century homes that by the 1930s had deteriorated to slum dwellings. By that time, all traces of former gardens had disappeared, and only the bare necessities were evident in the hard-packed

yards that remained. Shortly thereafter, the homes in this view were demolished and replaced by a public housing project. (Photograph by Peter Sekaer; courtesy of the Preservation Society of Charleston.)

A 1939 record of the garden at the Jenkins Mikell House, located at the corner of Rutledge and Montagu Streets in Charleston, is a study in contrasts. The imposing city home of I. Jenkins Mikell, a prominent Edisto Island planter, was surrounded by an interesting array of exotic garden plants. The small servants' quarters, while solid, appear to be strictly functional and without any garden ornamentation. Regardless of the size of any property, domestic functions had to be accommodated while ornamental gardens were a luxury before the days of modern plumbing and kitchens. (Photographs by Thomas T. Waterman; courtesy of the Library of Congress, Prints and Photographs Division, Historic American Buildings Survey.)

In 1907, at high tide, a sailboat could easily reach 9 Gibbes Street, a classic Charleston single house facing south with a dependency unusually placed at a right angle at the rear. The low, brick seawall bordered the yard where there was no evidence of a garden, and the board fence defines the property line, which extends north with a width sufficient for a drive to connect the home to Gibbes Street. (Courtesy of the T. Hunter McEaddy family.)

Prior to 1910 and the construction of Murray Boulevard, Gibbes Street was only one block long and turned west off Legare Street, ending at Lenwood Creek, a tributary of the Ashley River, as seen in this photograph from 1900. The earliest homes on this block dated to the late 18th and early 19th centuries, and those farther west were located directly along the water and marsh and separated from them by a low, brick seawall. Perhaps because of this low-lying position subject to saltwater flooding, there is little evidence of gardening in these views. When the Murray Boulevard project was completed, these properties were surrounded by landfill and effectively moved from the edge to the center of the lower peninsula, one block north of South Battery Street. (Courtesy of the T. Hunter McEaddy family.)

In 1910, tidal creeks and marshland along the Ashley River and adjacent historic neighborhoods south of Broad Street were filled in to form Murray Boulevard and create many additional blocks for development at the foot of the Charleston peninsula. This view shows a new residence and garden under construction on the resulting landfill, which became a large, new residential area bordering the city's oldest. (Photograph by Mary Barnwell Means; courtesy of the Preservation Society of Charleston.)

This view taken *c.* 1910 shows a dredge beginning to create landfill behind the seawall under construction to form Murray Boulevard. The Ashley River marsh was soon to give way to a large area of new homes and gardens built in the early to mid-20th century. (Photograph by Mary Barnwell Means; courtesy of the Preservation Society of Charleston.)

A view taken in 1910 showing construction of the Murray Boulevard seawall, which would turn marshes and creeks bordering the southern and western boundaries of the lower Charleston peninsula into filled land and ultimately blocks of new homes and gardens. Architectural and garden styles of the 20th century predominate in this area and provide interesting contrasts to adjacent streets filled with 18th- and 19th-century work. (Photograph by Franklin Frost Sams; courtesy of Historic Charleston Foundation.)

Before construction of Murray Boulevard in 1910, South Battery and Gibbes Streets terminated in marsh grass and mud flats along the Ashley River at the western edge of the peninsula. Because of proximity to the saltwater and frequent tidal flooding, gardening was a challenge in these yards, and there is little evidence in this view. When the Low Battery seawall and the boulevard were completed, a new neighborhood filled the former wetlands, and these older homes became landlocked. (Photograph by Franklin Frost Sams; courtesy of Historic Charleston Foundation.)

In a project similar to the creation of Murray Boulevard in 1910, Lockwood Drive was extended up the Ashley River from the end of Broad Street in the mid-20th century. Once again, a new neighborhood expanded the peninsula, this time along its western boundary, and the area was quickly built up with homes and gardens in the suburban style of the day. This area stood in sharp contrast to the large, 19th-century dwellings and gardens it abutted, and formerly waterfront properties became landlocked. (Photographs by H. Philip Staats; courtesy of Historic Charleston Foundation.)

Two

PIAZZAS

An early-20th-century view of the piazza at 43 Legare Street illustrates how comfortably these typical Charleston side porches connect single houses to their gardens and provide comfortable outdoor living areas. (Courtesy of Charlotte and Strait Fairey.)

A young lad takes his first steps on the family piazza overlooking a garden on Church Street in the 1940s. Even today, piazzas continue to be an integral part of Charleston homes and are commonly used for entertaining, visiting, and the more mundane aspects of life, just as they have been through the centuries. (Courtesy of Eva Ravenel.)

This single house on Legare Street was enhanced with flower boxes lining the piazza railings, providing colorful planting in the late-19th-century view. Color and unusual plants were particularly popular among gardeners during this period. (Courtesy of Historic Charleston Foundation, Detroit Photographic Company Collection.)

The Gadsden Morris House, located on East Bay Street just south of Calhoun Street, displayed a mid-20th-century addition to its handsome two-story piazzas. Screens helped make outdoor living even more enjoyable in the land of mosquitoes and "no-see-ums." (Photograph by Louis Schwartz; courtesy of Historic Charleston Foundation.)

The piazzas at 69 Church Street overlook a neighboring garden with an informal collection of plantings. (Courtesy of Historic Charleston Foundation.)

In 1958, the Dr. James Moultrie House at 20 Montagu Street was set in an overgrown, vine-filled garden that provided a private, shady bower for its west-facing piazzas. (Photograph by J. E. Boucher; courtesy of Library of Congress, Prints and Photographs Division, Historic American Buildings Survey.)

Rather than traditional piazzas, floor-to-ceiling windows open onto unroofed balconies with wrought-iron railings for viewing the large garden to the south at the Nathaniel Russell House at 51 Meeting Street. (Photograph by Clarke Photo; courtesy of Historic Charleston Foundation.)

Two young boys on scooters enjoyed space to play at 26 Parkwood Avenue near Hampton Park in 1927. As was also common in older neighborhoods, a trellis supported vines to provide shade and privacy for the piazza. Unlike in the older areas, however, these new neighborhoods tended to have larger lots with more room for play and gardening. A freestanding garage with drive for parking the family car had taken the place of stables and carriage houses by the time of this shot. (Courtesy of Historic Charleston Foundation, Eberle Collection.)

A nurse watches two children with bicycles in front of 15 Meeting Street. This 18th-century dwelling has unusual, rounded piazzas that open into a large side garden. (Photograph by *Art Work of Charleston*, W. H. Parish, publisher; courtesy of Historic Charleston Foundation.)

The piazza provided a cool spot for warm-weather living in the days before residential air-conditioning was common. Typically they faced south or east to capture the prevailing summer breezes and shade the interior from the sun. (Courtesy of Eva Ravenel.)

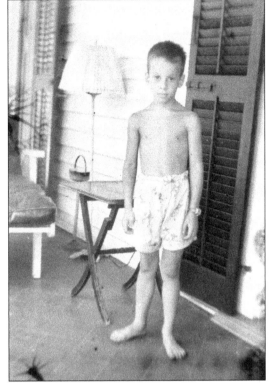

A large Charleston double house at 321 East Bay Street features side piazzas but no evidence of a garden in this 1950s picture. As neighborhoods declined, even if the homes survived, more fragile gardens often did not if care was lacking. (Photograph by H. Philip Staats; courtesy of Historic Charleston Foundation.)

A grandmother and a newborn enjoy the outdoor living space on the piazza of this Charleston single house. (Courtesy of Historic Charleston Foundation, Eberle Collection.)

Three

GATES, WALLS, AND ENTRANCES

This view through a handsome wrought-iron gate at 23 Legare Street reveals a single house set back from a brick wall with an elaborate planted garden and an unusual small cottage set at a right angle to the main house. Iron gates, often works of art in themselves, separate many Charleston gardens from the public realm. (Courtesy of Historic Charleston Foundation, Eberle Collection.)

A mid-19th-century single house is set slightly back from the street with room for a small front garden and a side drive leading to dependencies, such as stables and a kitchen house in the rear. Note the tall, wooden picket fence enclosing the property. (Photograph by Franklin Frost Sams; courtesy of Historic Charleston Foundation.)

A large, simple, wrought-iron gate opens to a narrow garden bordered to the left by the walls of a neighboring house. (Courtesy of Historic Charleston Foundation.)

This large, formerly elegant mansion on East Bay Street near the Market and its ample grounds show the ravages of war, Reconstruction, and hard times in the late 19th century. The fence surrounding the property is all that remains of the formerly grand gardens that it once protected. (Photograph by W. B. Austin; courtesy of Historic Charleston Foundation.)

A young miss shows off the latest fashions, c. 1922, in the family garden at 79 Fishburne Street at the intersection with St. Philip Street. A concrete walk and a border of annuals and perennials against the iron fence suggest a well-cared-for garden. (Courtesy of Historic Charleston Foundation, Eberle Collection.)

This residence near the western end of Tradd Street at number 172 is unusual for Charleston with its two-story portico and large columns. However, in this view, it faced a garden with common local plant material, including a live oak and palmetto as well as a fence of stucco with iron pickets. (Photograph by Lanneau's Art Store, publisher; courtesy of Historic Charleston Foundation.)

OLD GATES, MEETING STREET.   CHARLESTON, S. C.

Intricate wooden gates and massive masonry columns guard the garden at 15 Meeting Street. (Photograph by Lanneau's Art Store, publisher; courtesy of Historic Charleston Foundation.)

This large single house on Legare Street has flower-filled window boxes, vine-covered piazzas, and a small, formal garden visible through a tall gate. (Courtesy of Charlotte and Strait Fairey.)

71

This large, grand mansion at 69 Barre Street was surrounded by an ornate wooden fence, which rivaled the more common wrought-iron work found through the city. (Photograph by H. Philip Staats; courtesy of Historic Charleston Foundation.)

A small house without characteristic piazzas was built right against the city sidewalks at the corner of Archdale and Clifford Streets with no apparent room for a garden. The board fence to the rear probably concealed an area used for domestic chores in this 1936 photograph. (Photograph by Walker Evans; courtesy of Library of Congress, Prints and Photographs Division, FSA-OWI Collection.)

The Vanderhorst House, a large, imposing double house facing Chapel Street at number 28, was one of a number of similar homes on the east side of the peninsula north of Calhoun Street built in the early 19th century. In this view, a tall but simple wrought-iron picket fence encloses a front garden into which matching, semi-circular steps connect a single-story piazza. (Courtesy of Historic Charleston Foundation, Eberle Collection.)

This brick single house located at 37 New Street at the intersection with Broad Street shows only a rustic wood picket fence and no sign of a garden in this perspective. The home is identified as the residence of the photographer, Franklin Frost Sams, who took many of these pictures in the late 1890s. (Photograph by Franklin Frost Sams; courtesy of Historic Charleston Foundation.)

A snow scene near 170 Broad Street shows that simple, iron picket fences are in vogue to surround gardens in this scene from the early 20th century. Wooden barricades protect young street trees in this view. (Photograph by Franklin Frost Sams; courtesy of Historic Charleston Foundation.)

Multiple generations of a large family pose on the front lawn of their home at 48 Parkwood Avenue. It is interesting that a low clipped hedge, rather than the traditional Charleston fence, separates this garden from the public sidewalk. (Courtesy of Historic Charleston Foundation, Eberle Collection.)

This imposing residence south of Broad Street occupies most of the frontage of its lot, leaving room for carriage drives on either side. Tall, solid wooden gates provided complete privacy for the garden and dependencies located to the rear of the property. (Courtesy of Historic Charleston Foundation.)

A single house at 34 Coming Street has a one-story piazza overlooking a garden completely hidden from public view by a tall, solid board fence. A raised, brick sidewalk fronts the property, although the street is still unpaved in this late-19th- or early-20th-century view. The stone block on the sidewalk in front of the fence is a carriage step, used for stepping up into tall carriages. (Photograph by Franklin Frost Sams; courtesy of Historic Charleston Foundation.)

Contrasting drive and pedestrian gates open into a barren garden space that surely knew better days when it was new. (Courtesy of Historic Charleston Foundation.)

The piazzas of a double house facing the street are partially visible at 60 Hasell Street. It has a small garden in front and a dependency unusually placed on the street to form a partial enclosure. A large garden to the right appears to belong to a neighboring property, and both are enclosed by wrought-iron and masonry fences. Nursemaids and their charges in wicker carriages appear to be enjoying the scene in this late-19th-century picture. (Photograph by Franklin Frost Sams; courtesy of Historic Charleston Foundation.)

Tall, brick columns support wooden driveway and pedestrian gates leading into the rectory of St. Philip's Church on Church Street. (Courtesy of Historic Charleston Foundation.)

A fanciful, wrought-iron fence, arbor, and gate guard a garden on Meeting Street. (Courtesy of Historic Charleston Foundation.)

A view through a wrought-iron gate introduces an exceptionally large garden on South Battery Street. The design of this gate is very unusual and not at all like most of the beautiful, but more classical, ironwork found in Charleston. (Courtesy of Susanne and Tom Trainer.)

Massive brick and stucco steps make a fine growing medium for vines and ferns at the old rectory of St. Philip's Church. (Courtesy of Historic Charleston Foundation.)

The tree-lined entrance to Robert B. Rhett's plantation near Beaufort is typical of many plantations in the Lowcountry. This image from the 1860s shows the carefully aligned live oaks bordering the drive, which were planted by an earlier generation to create an impressive sense of arrival at the property. (Courtesy of Library of Congress, Prints and Photographs Division.)

Four

PUBLIC SPACES AND INSTITUTIONS

This block-long view shows dwellings representing a variety of architectural styles, each set back from the street to provide spaces for small gardens facing the street and White Point Gardens, a public park overlooking the Battery and Charleston Harbor. (Courtesy of Historic Charleston Foundation, Eberle Collection.)

Three ladies look down on the garden from the piazza of a residence on lower Legare Street near South Battery Street. Several palmetto trees are evident across the street in the garden to the left. (Photograph by *Art Work of Charleston*, W. H. Parish, publisher; courtesy of Historic Charleston Foundation.)

In the mid-20th century, a home on St. Michael's Alley, with no garden of its own, faced a ragged collection of plants belonging to a neighbor. (Courtesy of Historic Charleston Foundation.)

Cobblestoned Chalmers Street displayed a variety of architectural styles and ample evidence that vines could take over the city if given free reign, as seen in this picture from the 1940s. (Courtesy of Historic Charleston Foundation.)

This late-19th-century view down Beaufain Street shows a variety of fences surrounding gardens facing the street and wooden trellises to support ornamental vines. (Photograph by *Art Work of Charleston*, W. H. Parish, publisher; courtesy of Historic Charleston Foundation.)

With much of the Charleston peninsula just a few feet above sea level, it is not uncommon for gardens to suffer a saltwater inundation, especially during extra-high tides each spring and fall and, of course, during occasional hurricanes. Through the centuries, however, the gardens and their gardeners have proved resilient, and lush, sub-tropical growth continues to flourish. (Photograph by Franklin Frost Sams; courtesy of Historic Charleston Foundation.)

An 1865 photograph shows the mansions along East Battery Street looking remarkably as they do today except for dismantled cannons in the street and somewhat neglected gardens after years on the front lines facing the blockaded harbor. (Courtesy of the Library of Congress, Prints and Photograph Division.)

Since the invention of photography, rare snowfalls in Charleston seem to bring out amateur and professional cameras to record the scene. These homes on Calhoun Street were new when this picture was taken in the late 19th century, and the snow cover seems to make their young gardens appear even more immature. (Photograph by Franklin Frost Sams; courtesy of Historic Charleston Foundation.)

A scene along the Battery, taken in the 19th century, shows an eclectic collection of large homes facing the public park known as White Point Gardens. Of special interest to gardeners is the greenhouse, located between the two large homes. (Courtesy of the Library of Congress, Prints and Photograph Division.)

The Charleston peninsula has many narrow streets and alleys lined with smaller dwellings, many of which were once dependencies in the gardens of large homes facing the main thoroughfares. In the 20th century, a number of these properties, having access to the streets, were subdivided and sold for smaller residences. In modern times, others have been renovated and now have lovely, small gardens while others contain no land beyond the footprint of the building. (Photographs by Franklin Frost Sams; courtesy of Historic Charleston Foundation.)

Though narrow, some of Charleston's alleys contain grand homes. Others such as Bottle, Horlbeck, and Philadelphia Alleys often were lined with dependencies of larger properties that in some cases were subdivided and became slum dwellings in the latter part of the 19th century. (Photograph by Franklin Frost Sams; courtesy of Historic Charleston Foundation.)

The home at the corner of East and South Battery Streets has a spectacular view across the harbor, which appears to make up for the apparent lack of interest in developing the small, walled area where no planting is evident. (Photograph by *Art Work of Charleston*, W. H. Parish, publisher; courtesy of Historic Charleston Foundation.)

This panoramic shot was taken from the High Battery walk across White Point Gardens to the mansions along East and South Batteries. Large live oaks grace the older areas of the park, and newer plantings in the foreground appear to be crepe myrtles and palmettos. The park is bordered by a wide pedestrian path, benches, and memorabilia of the defense of Charleston during the War Between the States when the park was the closest point on the peninsula to the blockading Union forces. (Photograph by Haines Photo Company; courtesy of Library of Congress, Prints and Photograph Division.)

A young girl identified as Frances poses proudly in front of an equally young palmetto, the state tree, in White Point Gardens before the large live oaks, present in later years, were in evidence. (Photograph by Franklin Frost Sams; courtesy of Historic Charleston Foundation.)

Palmettos, oaks, ivy, and a grassy parade ground comprised the "garden" of the Porter Military Academy, a private secondary school for boys in the mid-20th century. (Courtesy of Historic Charleston Foundation.)

Two young ladies admire the bust of poet Henry Timrod erected in Washington Square Park. Although a public park, there is little evidence of the large trees or other plantings that would later turn this spot into a cool downtown sanctuary. (Photograph by Franklin Frost Sams; courtesy of Historic Charleston Foundation.)

The original Roper Hospital, located at Queen and Logan Streets in this 1865 view, appeared to have been carefully planted with a front garden, although it was no doubt neglected after years of siege. Shade trees are shown lining the street as they did throughout much of the city. (Courtesy of the Library of Congress, Prints and Photograph Division.)

Charlestonians strolled across a dike known as the West Point Mill Road, and youngsters drove their goat carts in an area that would later be filled in to expand the peninsula with the creation of Lockwood Drive in the middle of the 20th century. (Photograph by *Art Work of Charleston*, W. H. Parish, publisher; courtesy of Historic Charleston Foundation.)

This powder magazine is known as one of the oldest surviving structures in Charleston. Built *c.* 1719, it looks abandoned in this 1898 view when a natural "garden" of vines and other volunteers appeared to have taken over the premises. (Courtesy of Historic Charleston Foundation.)

A panoramic view of the original location of the Citadel, the military college of South Carolina, is shown in 1909 when Marion Square was a large, open parade ground with the tall column topped by a statue of South Carolina's 19th-century statesman John C. Calhoun as the park's most prominent feature. (Photograph by Haines Photo Company; courtesy of Library of Congress, Prints and Photograph Division.)

In 1909, a vista across Ashley River shows the open country that surrounded the city and the beautiful grove of live oaks that graced the grounds of the Charleston Country Club. (Photograph by Haines Photo Company; courtesy of Library of Congress, Prints and Photograph Division.)

In 1879, street vendors delivered their wares to the backyard of a Charleston garden where cooking and other domestic activities occurred. Most Charleston gardens were too small to grow food crops, so street vendors provided for a critical need for home food delivery in the days before supermarkets. (Photograph by Kilburn Brothers; courtesy of Library of Congress, Prints and Photographs Division.)

The elaborate grounds and architecture of the Charleston Orphan House were guarded by a Federal soldier in 1865. The gardens included clipped hedges and marble statuary and were among the grandest public grounds in the city. (Courtesy of the Library of Congress, Prints and Photograph Division.)

A panoramic view, taken in 1909, shows the large homes along East Battery Street and an open green in front of the Carolina Yacht Club. (Photograph by Haines Photo Company; courtesy of Library of Congress, Prints and Photograph Division.)

Elaborate gardens, statuary, and ornamental ponds surrounding islands were all part of the fanciful setting for Charleston's Inter-State and West Indian Exposition in 1902. The site was later developed by the city as Hampton Park, a large public garden that retained vestiges of the exposition's design. (Courtesy of the Library of Congress, Prints and Photograph Division.)

Five

BEACH HOUSES, RURAL RETREATS, AND PLANTATIONS

In the small pineland town of Summerville, north of Charleston, children played with a buggy at the start of the 20th century. Summerville was one of a number of Lowcountry communities settled as summer retreats for planters because of their perceived healthful locations away from marshlands and mosquitoes. Its rambling 19th-century homes occupied large lots filled with tall pines, live oaks, camellias, and azaleas. (Photograph by Franklin Frost Sams; courtesy of Historic Charleston Foundation.)

Stiles Point Plantation, located on James Island overlooking the harbor, is shown in this 1950s picture, at a time when suburban development was spreading into this formerly rural area. The beginnings of this home are thought to date back to 1745 and the structure shown was expanded in 1891. A large, multi-trunked sago palm and a crepe myrtle dominate the center of the bed fronting the piazza. Today nearly all of the farmlands that formerly bordered the city across its rivers and harbor now grow suburban homes. (Courtesy of the Preservation Society of Charleston.)

In the 19th and early 20th centuries, goat carts pulled by pet goats were popular with children in city and country. These youngsters appear to be riding on the spacious grounds of a plantation garden with the ever-present backdrop of large, moss-draped live oaks. (Courtesy of Lorraine and Frank Hanckel.)

This photograph of a small clubhouse in St. Andrews Parish west of the Ashley illustrates the typical natural flora of the countryside surrounding the Charleston peninsula across both the Ashley and Cooper Rivers. The predominant gardening philosophy seems to have been for nature to take its course. (Photograph by Franklin Frost Sams; courtesy of Historic Charleston Foundation.)

Even into the middle of the 20th century, leaving the peninsula city across either the Ashley or Cooper Rivers soon found one in open country with forests and working farms and plantations just beginning to see suburban encroachment. Coburg Dairy was one such prominent landmark on the Savannah Highway, where generations of the same family made their home. (Courtesy of Lorraine and Frank Hanckel.)

The family home at Coburg sits on a bluff overlooking a tidal creek and marsh with an informal country garden of azaleas and camellias shaded by large live oaks festooned with Spanish moss. (Photograph by Louis Schwartz; courtesy of Lorraine and Frank Hanckel.)

The small and more formal front entrance garden to the home at Coburg was planted with azaleas and boxwood and faced a long, oak-lined avenue that led in from the Savannah Highway to a parking court, as show in this 1930s view. (Courtesy of Lorraine and Frank Hanckel.)

As a working dairy farm, pastures and fields surrounded the small portion of Coburg property adjacent to the home, which was devoted to an ornamental garden. (Courtesy of Lorraine and Frank Hanckel.)

Though they look dressed for a stroll in the Coburg gardens, these ladies appear to be surveying the edge of the working farm. (Courtesy of Lorraine and Frank Hanckel.)

Many country homes were situated along creeks and rivers, which offered inviting opportunities for a cooling saltwater dip. Here the marsh grass had been cleared and an area enclosed to create a secure pool, complete with slides, clearly popular with all ages on a hot summer day in the Lowcountry. (Courtesy of Lorraine and Frank Hanckel.)

Brothers, sisters, cousins, and a young mother pose on a slide in this 1930s country garden. Unlike the confined spaces of many city gardens, those in the country had ample room for play equipment. In downtown Charleston, ancient garden walls could be climbed to provide connecting paths for exploring through backyards, while streets, parks, occasional playgrounds, and an ancient city meant for exploring and stimulating young imaginations proved to be ample substitutes. (Courtesy of Lorraine and Frank Hanckel.)

A 19th-century beach house on Sullivan's Island is typical. Although many Charlestonians escaped the city's summer heat by moving to the beach, ornamental gardening did not appear to have been a priority. A rustic picket fence and a lawn of native wildflowers served as the garden in this view, taken around 1900. Generally native beach shrubs, sea oats, palmettos, and sand were the other predominant landscape features. (Photograph by Franklin Frost Sams; courtesy of Historic Charleston Foundation.)

Simple fencing and whatever native growth would survive without care in the sandy soil typically surrounded this Sullivan's Island beach house, identified with the Gibbes family. (Photograph by Franklin Frost Sams; courtesy of Historic Charleston Foundation.)

In the 1940s, two young ladies posed at Edisto Beach showing off pictures of their favorite beaus. The beach houses in the background sat directly at the edge of the beach, surrounded by sand with no attempt to garden in sight. In the distance, a naturally occurring grove of palmettos, the South Carolina state tree, offer a bit of shade and the only greenery in view. (Courtesy of Lorraine and Frank Hanckel.)

The encroaching sand dunes plus a desire to relax and escape the heat probably discouraged any efforts to garden anything other than the sea oats and wildflowers that nature provided. (Photograph by Franklin Frost Sams; courtesy of Historic Charleston Foundation.)

Beach houses built in the 20th century on the Isle of Palms typically followed their older Sullivan's Island counterparts and relied upon native landscape. These contrast with contemporary practices, which often provide for elaborate landscaped gardens surrounding beach homes intended for year-round use as well as vacations. (Photograph by William M. Muckenfuss; courtesy of Historic Charleston Foundation.)

The garden of a family's beach house was one enormous sand box for this youngster on Edisto Beach. The ever-present and naturally occurring palmetto trees were the only plant material visible. In the present day, tastes have changed, and most beach houses have at least some green space and often elaborate gardens that have many of the native plants that will grow at the beach and even lush green lawns supported by irrigation systems. (Courtesy of Lorraine and Frank Hanckel.)

The ruin of a formerly handsome plantation house, which was rapidly slipping away, evokes memories. An old rose in bloom and a lone palmetto trunk seemed to be the only evidence of the gardens that presumably surrounded it at one time. (Photograph by H. Philip Staats; courtesy of Historic Charleston Foundation.)

Children of an Edisto Island plantation enjoyed playing outside in this happy scene photographed in the early 1900s against a background of fields and work sheds. (Courtesy of Gale Belser Thompson.)

A typical, moss-draped live oak avenue leading to Oakland Plantation was the predominant landscape feature in this picture taken in 1940. The home dates from 1740; many times, these majestic alleys are the sole surviving landscape feature in centuries-old country gardens. (Photograph by C. O. Greene; courtesy of Library of Congress, Prints and Photographs Division, Historic American Buildings Survey.)

Hampton Plantation was built around 1735 on Wambaw Creek near the Santee River in northern Charleston County. When this picture was taken some 200 years later, it was the home of Archibald Rutledge, noted South Carolina author and poet laureate. Pres. George Washington was a guest of the plantation during his Southern tour in the 1790s, and it is said that he argued

against removing what has become the large live oak to the right of the portico, Note that this early-20th-century view shows the plowed fields of a working farm approaching the front of the house. (Photograph by C. E. Peterson; courtesy of Library of Congress, Prints and Photographs Division, Historic American Buildings Survey.)

This 1970s view of the home at Seaside Plantation on Edisto Island shows informal plantings that appear to be azaleas, crepe myrtle, and yew surrounded by a large lawn shaded with oaks. (Photograph by Charles N. Bayless, AIA; courtesy of Library of Congress, Prints and Photographs Division, Historic American Buildings Survey.)

Boone Hall was a large working plantation on the outskirts of Mount Pleasant. This picture was taken in the 1930s and shows tile-roofed, brick quarters for former slaves that were located between the gardens of the big house and the fields. (Photograph by Frances Benjamin Johnston; courtesy of Library of Congress, Prints and Photographs Division, Frances Benjamin Johnston Collection.)

In 1862, these slave quarters were a significant part of the grounds of a plantation located at Port Royal south of Charleston. (Photograph by Timothy H. O'Sullivan; courtesy of Library of Congress, Prints and Photographs Division.)

Fenwick Hall Plantation, built in 1750, is an imposing brick country house on Johns Island. This view shows an avenue of mature palmettos bordered by live oaks and magnolias leading to the house from a wrought-iron gate bordered by brick columns and a wall. It was typical of plantation homes to have a tree-lined drive approaching the main house. (Courtesy of Library of Congress, Prints and Photographs Division, Historic American Buildings Survey.)

In these scenes, it is difficult to imagine that this home of the William Seabrook Plantation on Edisto Island, handsome even in decline, had once been the center of a vast sea island cotton empire and was surrounded by acres of elegant gardens where the Marquis de Lafayette was entertained during a visit in the 1820s. (Courtesy of the T. Hunter McEaddy family.)

By the 1920s, just a few hearty shrubs remain to indicate the elaborate gardens that once surrounded this decaying home at Seabrook Plantation on Edisto Island. Occupation by Union troops during the War Between the States and years of poverty during Reconstruction and the decades that followed had taken their toll. (Courtesy of the T. Hunter McEaddy family.)

By the 1920s, the big house of the William Seabrook Plantation on Edisto Island had been reduced to near ruin with all vestiges of former gardens destroyed. In the 1930s and 1940s, the property was lovingly restored and elaborate gardens re-created the ambience of its antebellum heyday when its outlying fields grew lucrative crops of the famed sea island cotton. (Photograph by C. O. Greene; courtesy of Library of Congress, Prints and Photographs Division, Historic American Buildings Survey.)

In addition to the inevitable live oaks filled with Spanish moss, the double drive approaching the house of the William Seabrook Plantation was lined with privet hedges surrounding a lawn displaying statuary. The tall plants at the house are native yaupon hollies. The view of the rear shows intricate parterres filled with annuals and crossing paths with beds of camellias and azaleas bordering. (Photograph by Charles N. Bayless, AIA; courtesy of Library of Congress, Prints and Photographs Division, Historic American Buildings Survey.)

Snee Farm, c. 1750, near Mount Pleasant, was the country home of Charles Pinckney, a framer of
the U.S. Constitution and noted patriot and statesman. In this 1940 view, the simple vernacular
architecture of the house, typical of many small plantation homes of the period, was planted
with evergreen shrubbery (perhaps camellias) and framed with live oaks. Like others in the

area, this home hosted President Washington during his Southern tour. (Photograph by C. O. Greene; courtesy of Library of Congress, Prints and Photographs Division, Historic American Buildings Survey.)

Many country homes relied upon ancient, moss-draped live oaks, native to the Lowcountry, as a primary garden feature. They were often underplanted with azaleas and camellias. This style remains popular today, particularly in the countryside, from the grandest to the most humble gardens. (Photograph by William M. Muckenfuss; courtesy of Historic Charleston Foundation.)

INDEX

Visit us at
arcadiapublishing.com

....

CPSIA information can be obtained
at www.ICGtesting.com
Printed in the USA
LVHW060839300422
717620LV00005B/26

9 781531 633110